THIS LAND CALLED AMERICA: INDIANA

CREATIVE EDUCATION

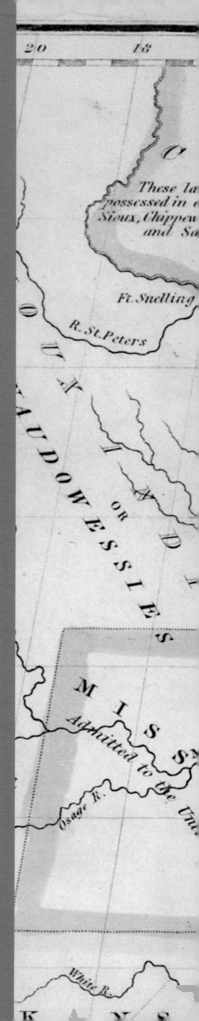

Published by Creative Education
P.O. Box 227, Mankato, Minnesota 56002
Creative Education is an imprint of The Creative Company
www.thecreativecompany.us

Book and cover design by Blue Design (www.bluedes.com)
Art direction by Rita Marshall
Printed in the United States of America

Photographs by Alamy (GEORGE AND MONSERRATE SCHWARTZ),
Corbis (Andy Altenburger/Icon SMI, Bettmann, Jerry Cooke, Richard
Cummins, FREIBERT/CORBIS SYGMA), Getty Images (Altrendo
Nature, Currier and Ives, Melissa Farlow, Tim Fitzharris, John Fleck,
Bruce Forster, General Photographic Agency, Bernard Hoffman/Time
& Life Pictures, Harry How, Wendy Kaveney, Wallace Kirkland//Time
Life Pictures, David Muench, Frank Oliver, Panoramic Images, Henry
Cheever Pratt, Roy Toft/National Geographic)

Library of Congress Cataloging-in-Publication Data
Shofner, Shawndra.
Indiana / by Shawndra Shofner.
p. cm. — (This land called America)
Includes bibliographical references and index.
ISBN 978-1-58341-639-6
1. Indiana—Juvenile literature. I. Title. II. Series.
F526.3.S55 2008
977.2—dc22   2007019622

First Edition
9 8 7 6 5 4 3 2 1

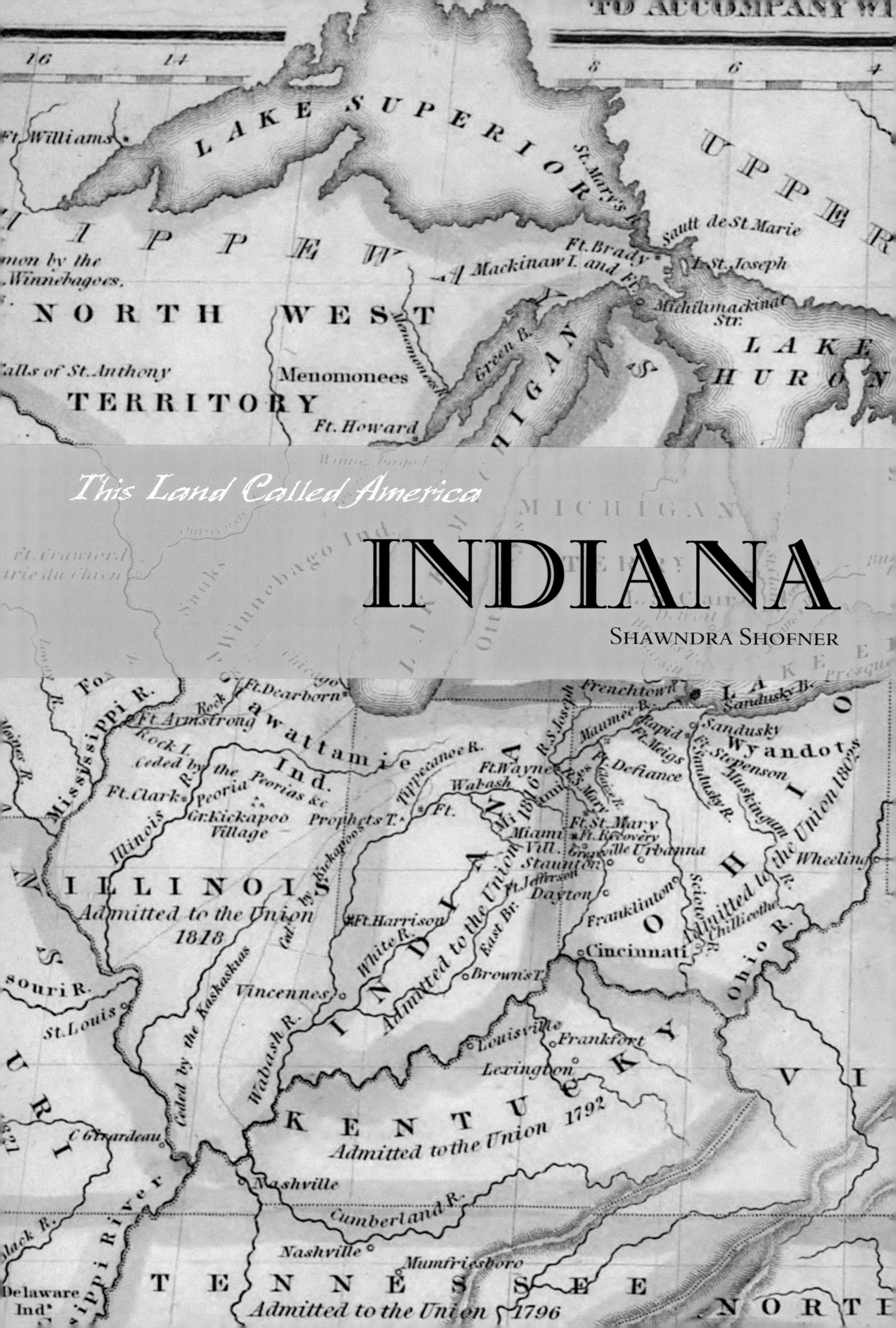

This Land Called America

INDIANA

Shawndra Shofner

THIS LAND CALLED AMERICA

Indiana

SHAWNDRA SHOFNER

MORE THAN 400,000 FANS GO WILD AS THE
PURDUE UNIVERSITY MARCHING BAND PLAYS
THE FIRST NOTES OF "BACK HOME IN INDIANA."
THE SONG RINGS THROUGH THE AIR, WHILE
THOUSANDS OF COLORFUL BALLOONS FLOAT TO
THE SKY. THIRTY-THREE OPEN-WHEELED CARS
WAIT BEHIND THE STARTING LINE OF THE 2.5-
MILE (4 KM) OVAL OF THE INDIANAPOLIS MOTOR
SPEEDWAY. ENGINES REV, AND EXHAUST FILLS
THE AIR AS THE DRIVERS WAIT IMPATIENTLY FOR
THE GREEN START FLAG TO DROP. THESE ARE
THE MOMENTS LEADING UP TO THE INDY 500,
THE LARGEST ONE-DAY SPORTING EVENT IN THE
WORLD, HELD EVERY MEMORIAL DAY WEEKEND IN
INDIANAPOLIS, INDIANA.

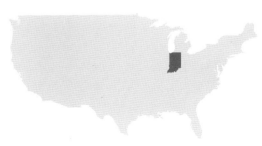

YEAR

1679 European explorer René-Robert de La Salle canoes down the St. Joseph River into Indiana.

EVENT

Territory Tamed

FOR THOUSANDS OF YEARS, AMERICAN INDIANS FROM
THE MIAMI, POTAWATOMI, DELAWARE, AND SHAWNEE
TRIBES LIVED IN INDIANA'S WOODLANDS AND PRAIRIES.
THE INDIAN MEN HUNTED DEER, RABBITS, AND BEARS.
FROM FRESHWATER LAKES, RIVERS, AND STREAMS, THEY
FISHED FOR CATFISH AND PIKE. THEY ALSO TRAPPED
BEAVERS, MUSKRATS, AND OTTERS. WOMEN GATHERED

René-Robert de La Salle

Explorer René-Robert de La Salle (above) did not travel as far south into Indiana as where the Hoosier National Forest (opposite) is today.

apples and nuts, cooked the meat over fires, and made clothing out of animal skins and furs.

In 1679, French explorer René-Robert de La Salle discovered Indiana. He and his party paddled canoes along the St. Joseph River and camped where the river bends south—at the present-day city of South Bend. After finding a route to the Mississippi via the Kankakee River, La Salle claimed Indiana and all land west from the Mississippi River to the Rocky Mountains and north from the Gulf of Mexico to Canada for France. He named the territory Louisiana after France's King Louis XIV.

YEAR

1732 Fort Vincennes becomes the first permanent settlement in Indiana.

EVENT

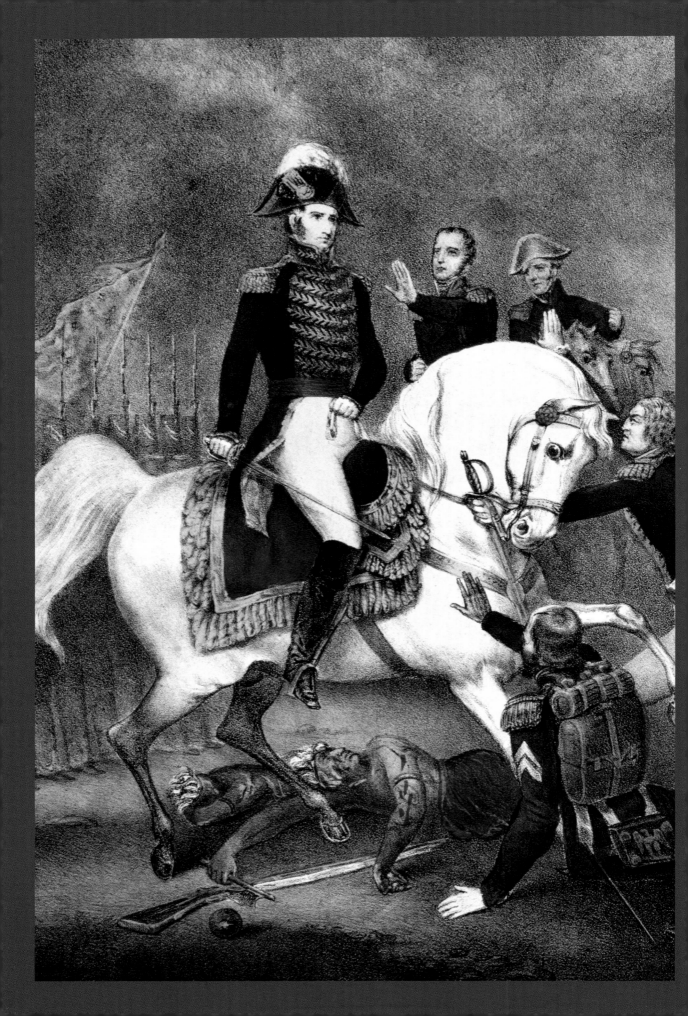

French fur traders and soldiers set up many forts in Indiana, including Fort Vincennes in 1732. French settlers built log homes and planted farms and orchards nearby. Soon, Indiana's oldest city—Vincennes—was founded.

France and England both wanted control of the fur trade in North America. In the French and Indian Wars of 1754–1763, some Indians fought with French soldiers to keep the English from taking over their land. But England won and claimed most of France's land in North America, including Indiana. The English also built forts to guard their claims, including one at Vincennes, which was called Fort Sackville.

Most of the American Revolutionary War, which began in 1775, was fought in the 13 colonies. However, American general George Rogers Clark and his men, who called themselves the "Big Knives," raided forts guarded by English soldiers in Indiana, including Fort Sackville, in 1779. England lost the war and gave its lands west and north of the Ohio River to the United States. This land, which included Indiana, became the Northwest Territory in 1787.

The U.S. government established the Indiana Territory in 1800. It included all of the land in the Northwest Territory except Ohio and part of Michigan. The next year, President John Adams named former soldier and politician William

Before he became a territorial governor and the ninth U.S. president, William H. Harrison fought Indians.

YEAR

1752   A smallpox epidemic strikes the American Indian population in Indiana, killing hundreds.

EVENT

The fertile farmlands located near Indiana's rivers attracted early settlers to the territory.

Henry Harrison as governor of the Indiana Territory. After the forming of the Michigan Territory in 1805 and the Illinois Territory in 1809, the boundaries of the Indiana Territory changed to become what the state's are today.

Settlers from nearby states came to the new territories looking for cheap farmland. So did people from Germany and Ireland. The natives tried to protect their lands from the new settlers. Shawnee chief Tecumseh and his brother, the Shawnee Prophet, lost the Battle of Tippecanoe in 1811 and the Battle of the Thames in 1813 against American troops led by Harrison. Once the Indians had been defeated, more settlers eagerly moved west. In 1816, Indiana became the 19th state, with the southern city of Corydon as its capital.

More and more people settled in Indiana, but they no longer stayed in the southern part of the state. They found rich farmland in northern Indiana, too. The state capital was moved to Indianapolis in 1821, and by the mid-1800s, the city had become the cultural and industrial center of the state.

YEAR

1812   General "Mad Anthony" Wayne, known for his wild behavior in battle, founds Fort Wayne.

EVENT

Tecumseh.

Dunes, Plains, and Hills

Indiana is called a Great Lakes state because Lake Michigan forms part of its northwestern border. The state of Michigan is on its northeastern border. To its east is Ohio, and to its west is Illinois. The Ohio River forms Indiana's southern border with Kentucky.

Five counties in Indiana's northwest corner are considered suburbs of Chicago, Illinois. The area is known for its steel mills, chemical refineries, and manufacturing plants. Gary, Indiana, is the largest city in the region. It is 25 miles (40 km) from Chicago and borders Lake Michigan. Indianapolis, the state's capital and its most populous city, is located in the central part of the state.

Gary may be the largest city in northwestern Indiana, but Indianapolis (above) is the largest in the state.

For 30 miles (48 km) along Lake Michigan's coast from Michigan City to Gary, grand sand dunes rise next to the waterswept shore. This area is the Indiana Dunes National Lakeshore. There, Karner blue butterflies flit among bearberry bushes and prickly pear cactus. The desert-like terrain includes Mount Tom, a dune that reaches a height of 192 feet (58 m), and the 123-foot-tall (37 m) Mount Baldy. A "living dune," Mount Baldy shifts its position every year due to the strong winds that come off the lake. In the grasslands and forests just beyond the dunes, coyotes slink beneath towering white pines, while downey woodpeckers knock on the trees.

Part of Indiana's border with Lake Michigan is designated as Indiana Dunes National Lakeshore.

YEAR
1842   The University of Notre Dame is founded in South Bend by Reverend Edward Sorin.
EVENT

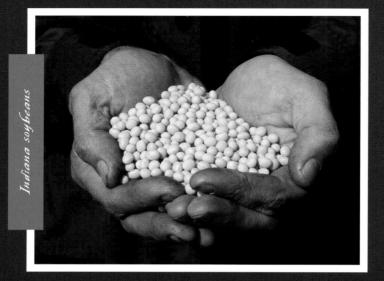

South of the lakeshore are Indiana's Great Lakes Plains. These plains make up the northern third of Indiana. The rich, low-lying land is also found in Wisconsin, Illinois, and Ohio. There are many small hills, lakes, and bogs in this area that are home to least terns, Canada lynx, and Indiana bats. Farmers grow potatoes, soybeans, wheat, rye, and corn in the rich black soil. They also raise beef and dairy cattle, sheep, and poultry.

Covering the middle third of the state is an area called the Till Plains. The mostly flat land contains the highest point in Indiana. Hoosier Hill, at 1,257 feet (383 m), is 11 miles (18 km)

Soybeans (above) are an important crop in Indiana and are grown primarily in the Great Lakes Plains, a region just south of Indiana Dunes National Lakeshore (opposite).

1847   Missionary John Chapman, popularly known as Johnny Appleseed, dies in Allen County.

During the Great Depression of the 1930s, farmers in Indiana allowed advertisers to paint giant ads on their barns.

Brown County Barn

north of the city of Richmond in the east-central part of the state. Many farms dot the plains, which are known for producing some of the state's best farmland. Some farmers grow oats, soybeans, apples, and peaches. Others raise hogs and cattle. There are also coal mines in the area's east and oil wells in the west.

Farms, coal mines, oil wells, and limestone quarries fill out much of Indiana's Southern Plains and Lowlands in the southern third of the state. The 200,000-acre (80,937 ha) Hoosier National Forest in south-central Indiana features caves, canyons, and bluffs beneath its towering hickory, oak, and hemlock trees. Turkey vultures and hawks coast on the wind, while catfish and crappies swim in the Ohio River. White-tailed deer, raccoons, opossums, foxes, and skunks are a few of the many wild animals that make their homes in the steep hills called "The Knobs" along the Ohio River.

Mild winters and humid summers are typical in Indiana. In the winter, temperatures range from 26 to 34 °F (-3 to 1 °C). Snow falls in all parts of the state, but blizzards and heavy snowfalls are more common in the north. March and April bring frequent thunderstorms and tornadoes. Summer temperatures average around 75 °F (24 °C).

Foxes thrive in the wooded areas of southern Indiana, feeding on small animals such as mice.

YEAR
1868   Indiana's most infamous outlaws, the Reno Gang, hold up a train and escape with $96,000.
EVENT

Pioneers and Entrepreneurs

MANY PEOPLE FROM OHIO, KENTUCKY, AND THE EAST
COAST MOVED TO INDIANA AFTER IT BECAME A STATE
IN 1816. OTHERS CAME FROM THE SOUTH TO ESCAPE
SLAVERY. THESE PIONEERS FARMED THE LAND, HELPED
EACH OTHER CHOP DOWN TREES, BUILT BARNS, AND
MADE ROADS. AS MORE WHITE PEOPLE SETTLED IN

Indiana, American Indians from the Delaware, Potawatomi, and Miami tribes moved farther west.

Farming was Indiana's major industry until the early 20th century. Then two of the natural resources used to make steel—iron ore and limestone—were found in great supply in Indiana. This changed the state forever. Steel mills and manufacturing plants soon became the state's biggest moneymakers.

James Oliver, a plow maker, founded the South Bend Iron Works plant in 1868. The plant produced the Oliver Chilled Plow, which was stronger and lasted longer than the

According to the 1920 census, a farm in Whitehall marked the center of the country's population.

Indiana farmers continued their steady production of crops, even after the steel boom.

At the Studebaker Company's headquarters in South Bend, people took care to design quality cars.

cast-iron plows farmers had used before. By the early 1900s, Indiana manufacturers were also producing cars in more than 40 cities. One of the largest outfits was the Studebaker Company, at which brothers Clement, Henry Jr., John, and Jacob Studebaker started building electric-powered cars in 1902 and gasoline-powered cars in 1904.

In 1901, banker J. P. Morgan, lawyer Elbert H. Gary, and businessman Andrew Carnegie merged their interests and founded the U.S. Steel Company. They built a new steel mill on Indiana's sand dunes beside Lake Michigan. Other businesses quickly moved to the area to supply goods and services to the mill and its employees. The city that developed around the company was named Gary after one of U.S. Steel's founders.

YEAR	
1907	Popcorn pioneer Orville Redenbacher is born in Clay County, Indiana.
EVENT	

In Fort Wayne, pilot Blanche S. Scott becomes the first woman to fly professionally.

Along with South Bend and Gary, the cities of Hammond, Fort Wayne, Elkhart, Anderson, Evansville, and Kokomo make up a region that is focused on industry.

The Amish of northern Indiana, who came from Pennsylvania in the 1840s, work hard and lead simple lives.

Most medicines in the 1800s were tonics sold by traveling salesmen. Such mixtures rarely did what they promised. In May 1896, a chemist named Eli Lilly founded a drug company in Indianapolis that made medicines based on science and research. He required that his medicines be given only by the order of a doctor. Lilly's mission also included discovering new and better medicines. Today, Eli Lilly and Company researches and tests drugs in more than 50 countries around the world.

Jobs in Indiana's many manufacturing plants and mills lured people to the state in the late 1800s and early 1900s from Germany, Ireland, Poland, Hungary, Belgium, and Italy. A group of religious people from North Carolina called Quakers settled in Richmond in the east-central part of the state. People from Switzerland and Germany seeking the freedom to practice Amish and Mennonite religious traditions settled in northeastern Indiana. African Americans from southern states migrated to Indiana to escape racist practices and low-paying hard labor in cotton fields.

YEAR

1920   The first game of the National Negro Baseball League is played in Indianapolis.

EVENT

oday, most of Indiana's population lives in or near the state's largest cities of Gary, Indianapolis, and Evansville. Many people work in car, truck, or transportation equipment factories and steel mills. More than 13,000 people work at Eli Lilly, and that is only one of the many chemical and drug companies that employ Indianans. About one-third of the state's population lives in rural areas. There, farmers raise animals for food and dairy or grow fruits, vegetables, and grains.

The high-powered industrial world of Indiana's cities, represented by such businesses as Eli Lilly and Company (above), is sharply contrasted with the state's peaceful rural areas (opposite).

1958   Popular singer and entertainer Michael Jackson is born in Gary.

Inside Indiana

HOLIDAYS ARE CELEBRATED EVERY DAY IN THE SOUTHWEST-ERN TOWN OF SANTA CLAUS, INDIANA. ON AUGUST 3, 1946, LOUIS J. KOCH, AN INDUSTRIALIST FROM EVANSVILLE AND FATHER OF NINE CHILDREN, OPENED SANTA CLAUS LAND, THE WORLD'S FIRST THEME PARK. CHILDREN COULD RIDE THE MOTHER GOOSE LAND TRAIN, VISIT A TOY FACTORY WITH ELVES AT WORK, AND TALK TO SANTA CLAUS. THE ENTIRE

town exhibits the holiday theme. For example, people can shop at the Kringle Place Shopping Center, camp at Lake Rudolph, or visit the 22-foot-tall (7 m) Santa Claus statue just west of the city along Highway 245.

Wyandotte Cave is one of the largest limestone caverns in the world. It is located near the Ohio River in Indiana's south-central Crawford County. The cave has 25 miles (40 km) of passageways that are home to bats, salamanders, and crickets. Monument Mountain, a 135-foot (41 m) underground mountain, is found inside the cave, too.

Remains of a Mississippian Indian village from A.D. 1100–1450 are located near Evansville along the Ohio River. The 603-acre (244 ha) wildlife preserve is called Angel Mounds Historic Site. At the Voices of the East gathering every May, visitors get to see what life might have been like for these early natives. People dressed in clothing of the time act out scenes from daily life, recreating a working village. Typical homes of the time, such as the canvas wigwam, cattail mat lodge, and bark open lodge are on display for people to walk through.

Ordinary citizens (opposite) are proud of their beautiful capitol (above) in Indianapolis, which was constucted out of Indiana limestone in 1888.

From Evansville, people can look across the grand Ohio River and see the state of Kentucky.

The Indiana Territory's first governor, William Henry Harrison, built a grand mansion in Vincennes in 1804. He called the two-story brick home Grouseland because there were so many grouse, or game birds, living in the area. Chief Tecumseh, explorers Lewis and Clark, and former first lady Eleanor Roosevelt were a few of the distinguished people who visited the mansion. Harrison went on to become the ninth president of the U.S. But he died one month after taking office in 1851.

Race cars and college athletics dominate the sports scene in Indiana. The 559-acre (226 ha) Indianapolis Motor Speedway, which can seat 400,000 people, is the world's largest sporting facility. It was built in 1909 and has hosted more than 200 races. In addition to the annual Indy 500, other racing series such as Formula One, NASCAR, and Craftsman Truck take place at the track.

Indiana University's Hoosiers, wearing crimson and cream jerseys, compete in more than 20 sports. The Fighting Irish from the University of Notre Dame at South Bend draw college football fans from around the country. Coach Knute Rockne became a legend at Notre Dame. From 1918 to 1930, Rockne led the team to 105 wins, the greatest winning record in college football history.

YEAR
1988   Indiana senator Dan Quayle runs for vice president on George Bush's presidential ticket.
EVENT

Fans pack the stands at Notre Dame Stadium to witness the winning tradition of the Fighting Irish.

YEAR

2001

EVENT

The Notre Dame women's basketball team beats Purdue 66–44 for the national championship.

- 29 -

QUICK FACTS

Population: 6,313,520

Largest city: Indianapolis (pop. 783,438)

Capital: Indianapolis

Entered the union: December 11, 1816

Nickname: Hoosier State

State flower: peony

State bird: cardinal

Size: 36,418 sq mi (94,322 sq km)—38th-biggest in U.S.

Major industries: iron, steel, oil, agriculture, transportation equipment

Indiana is home to professional sports teams as well. The Indiana Pacers play in the National Basketball Association at their home arena of Conseco Fieldhouse. The Indianapolis Colts, led by star quarterback Peyton Manning, play in the National Football League. The Colts won the Super Bowl in 2007.

The people of Indiana today display the same hard-working, entrepreneurial spirit as the first pioneers to the state. Natural resources, great places for recreation, and the thrill of sports will continue to make a bright future for the industrious state of Indiana.

YEAR

2005 Indiana, Kentucky, and Tennessee are struck by more than 32 tornadoes.

EVENT

- 31 -

BIBLIOGRAPHY

Bockenhauer, Mark H., and Stephen F. Cunha. *National Geographic: Our Fifty States*. Washington: National Geographic, 2004.

Heinrichs, Ann. *Indiana*. Danbury, Conn.: Children's Press, 2000.

Kaercher, Dan. *Best of the Midwest: Rediscovering America's Heartland*. Guilford, Conn.: Globe Pequot Press, 2005.

Marshall, Richard, et al. *Explore America*. Washington, D.C.: AAA Publishing, 1996.

Northern Indiana Historical Society. "Indiana History." Northern Indiana Center for History. http://www.centerforhistory.org/indiana_history_maincontents.html.

Zenfell, Martha. *Insight Guide United States: On the Road*. Long Island City, N.Y.: Langenscheidt Publishing Group, 2001.

INDEX